rainbows

It's Sunny

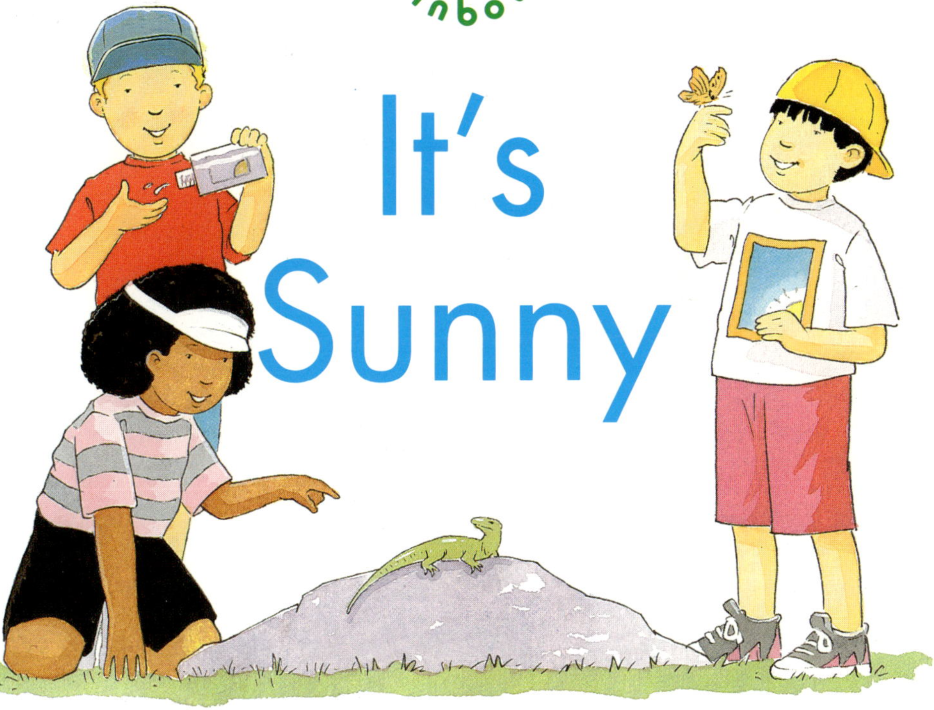

Helena Ramsay and
Paul Humphrey

Illustrated by
Stuart Trotter

Evans

It's a lovely sunny day.
The sky is blue and
there are no clouds.

We'd better wear sunhats, too.
Let's go for a walk.

We only see shadows outside on sunny days. The sun can't shine through you so it casts a shadow shaped like you on the ground.

That's because the sun is lower in the sky and this casts the shadow out further.

These flowers weren't open yesterday.

They have opened in the light and warmth of the sun. Their beautiful colours make them look attractive to insects.

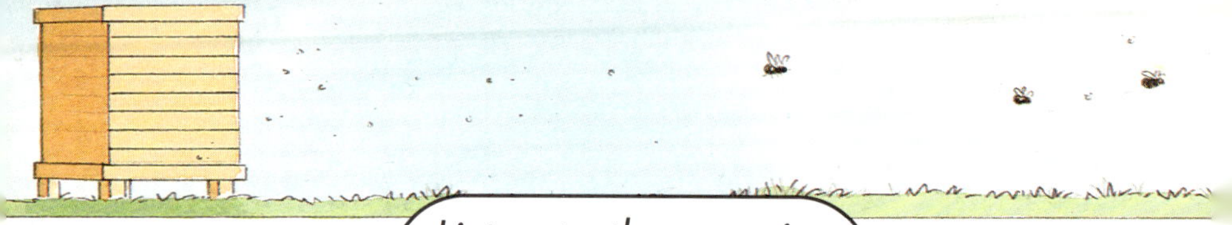

They are busy collecting nectar and pollen inside the flowers. They will carry them home to make honey.

Honey bees do, but wild bees make their own homes in the trunks of trees or in the ground.

Dragonflies spend the first two to three years of their life living under water. They look very different then and are called larvae.

They climb out of the water and change into the dragonflies that we know.

This one has only just changed. You can see its old skin near to it.

It is feeding on the sweet nectar inside the flower. Butterflies need sunlight to open the flowers so that they can feed.

It is laying its eggs on the underside of the leaf. What will they be when they hatch?

Look at the lizard lying on that rock.

Lizards are reptiles. Their bodies do not stay warm all the time, like ours do. They need to warm up in the sunshine so that they have the energy to move about.

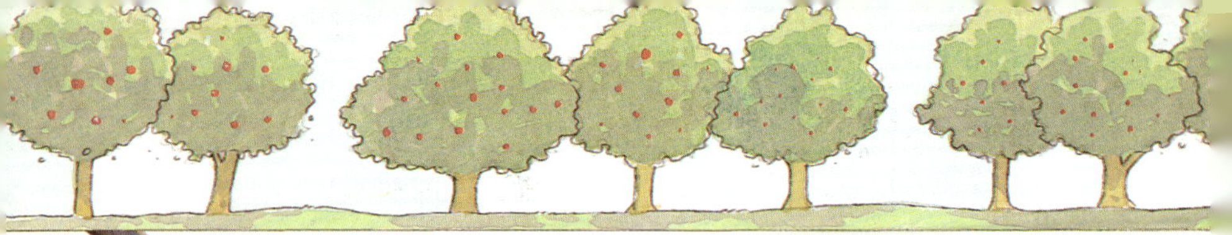

We depend on the sun too. Without the sun fruit and vegetables would never get ripe enough for us to eat them. Can you think of anything else that the sun ripens?

That's right, wheat has to ripen before it can be harvested and turned into flour to make bread.

He's having a bath. When it is hot and dry there aren't any puddles for him to wash in and so he has a dustbath instead.

When he shakes the dust away he shakes the bugs out, too.

Sweating is your body's way of keeping cool. Water comes out of tiny holes in your skin and that cools you down.

You get thirsty because your body has to replace the water that you sweat out. Let's buy a cold drink.

That's a good idea. If we get out of the sun we won't feel nearly so hot.

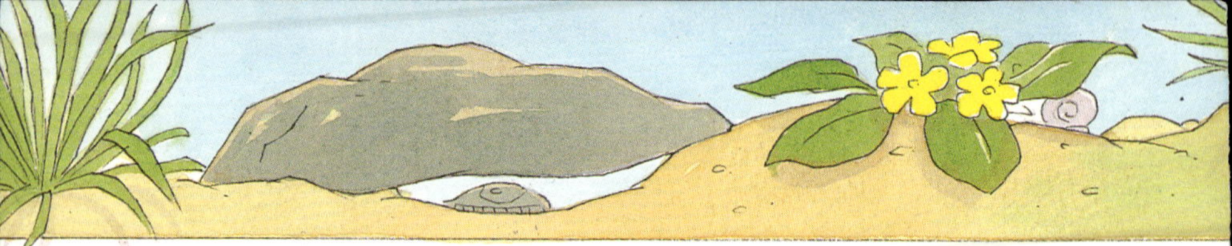

We must take care not to get sunburnt. On hot days like this we should wear sun cream to protect our skins.

Slugs and snails have to protect themselves from the sun, too. They only come out when it is cool and damp. Where do they hide on sunny days?

Let's go home now.
Look at our house.
It's shimmering.

That's caused by the heat rising off the ground. It's called a heat haze.

Yippee! Dad's filled the paddling pool.

Now we can really cool down.

All the animals and plants on this page need the sun. Can you name them all? The answers are printed below, but don't peep until you have tried yourself.

1. Dragonfly 2. Bee 3. Wheat 4. Snake 5. Butterfly 6. Tortoise 7. Apple 8. Lizard 9. Flowers

Winter Hands

Annie Clarkson

Shadow Train Books